MR. SILLY'S FRIEND

Quotations From Chainsaw Mike

TORONTO: ECW PRESS

This book has been published without the assistance of
the Ontario Development Corporation (cancelled, 1995), the
Ontario Publishing Centre (terminated, 1995), and the Ontario Arts
Council (cut by 40% in the first two years of the Harris regime).
Any resemblance to persons living or braindead is purely satirical.

PHOTO CREDITS: Front cover, Nigel Dickson; back cover, *The Toronto Sun*/
Chris Wahl; page 4, *The Toronto Star*/P. Power; page 12, *The Globe and Mail*/
T. Kolley; page 20, *The Toronto Star*/C. McConnell; page 26, Canapress/Tom
Hanson; page 32, *The Toronto Star*/B. Spremo; page 38, *The Toronto Sun*/Chris
Wahl; page 46, *The Globe and Mail*/Ed Regan; page 52, *Canapress*/Frank Gunn.

Illustrations copyright © Lind Design.

CANADIAN CATALOGUING IN PUBLICATION DATA

Harris, Mike, 1945–
Mr. Silly's friend: quotations from chainsaw Mike

ISBN 1-55022-343-7

1. Harris, Mike, 1945– – Quotations.   1. Title.

FC3077.1.H3A5 1997   971.3′04′092   C97-931521-2
F1058.H37 1997

Distributed in Canada by General Distribution Services,
30 Lesmill Road, Don Mills, Ontario M3B 2T6.

Published by ECW PRESS,
2120 Queen Street East, Suite 200,
Toronto, Ontario M4E 1E2.

http://www.ecw.ca/press

CONTENTS

SENSITIVE MIKE

MANSBRIDGE: Here's a last look now at tonight's top news stories. Ontario elected a Progressive Conservative government tonight, tossing out the NDP and opting for promises of tax cuts and tougher rules for welfare recipients.

MIKE HARRIS: We have much to do together, in the weeks and in the months ahead. For those who are currently trapped in a welfare system that demoralizes and despairs, we will work to restore independence and dignity and hope.

CROWD: Hurray!

(CBC News, 8 June 1995)

"Homelessness [is] generally people who have made a decision — and for whatever reason we regret they make it."

(*Toronto Star*, 2 April 1996)

"Certainly I would say there are some people living on the streets who have made that choice because we have quite a few dollars available for them," said Harris, adding it's a "major challenge" for his government.

(*Toronto Star*, 2 April 1996)

"I think times are tough. I think some of the adjustments of this sort of [previous] government policy of state of dependency and a transition to more self-reliance has had an impact on food banks. . . . We acknowledge that. We hope it's temporary. Our goal is to diminish the need for food banks in the long term," he said, adding that his own family dropped off a food donation at a fire hall the day before.

(*Toronto Star*, 2 April 1996)

Responding to criticism the tax savings are blood money generated by social service cuts, Harris told reporters that those uncomfortable with receiving the money may donate it to charity.

"If there are some people who have money that is more than they feel they need and they would like to see that go to a worthwhile cause, gosh, we really encourage that," he said.

(*Toronto Star*, 1 May 1996)

"I can't tell you how many millionaires started out with minimum-wage jobs."

(*Toronto Star*, 19 September 1995)

More households with two working parents, not the government's 21.6 percent cut in welfare rates, is the main reason more children are going to school hungry, Premier Mike Harris says.

"If you go back 30 or 40 years ago, where it seemed to be that mom was in the kitchen with a hot breakfast cooking as everybody woke up in the morning, that's not the normal situation today," Harris told a news conference on the front steps of the Legislature as he kicked off a breakfast program.

"There's been no particular link between children hungry in school and the unemployment rates or the welfare rates that are there. . . . Certainly, lifestyle changes contributed to it."

Those comments outraged New Democrat Marilyn Churley (Riverdale). Then, as she was condemning Harris in the Legislature, backbench Tory MPP Joe Spina snapped at her, "Why don't you go home and take care of your own kids?" ☞

Churley, who raised her now-grown daughter on her own, said the comments by Harris and Spina "belittle women" and make it clear they don't see women as equal.

"They've exposed themselves for the sexists that they are," Churley said in an interview. "It just falls short of telling women they should be barefoot and pregnant and in the kitchen."

Spina (MPP for Brampton North) withdrew the comments after Churley protested.

"It was just in the heat of debate," Spina told reporters.

But asked if more children were going to school hungry not due to welfare cuts but because fewer mothers stayed at home, Spina said, "Well, that is true."

(*Toronto Star*, 7 November 1996)

Equal opportunity Mike: "Now here is a disabled person only 50% as good as an able-bodied worker but you must hire them and pay them as much as an able-bodied person. That's nonsense. Why should that employer. It doesn't make sense."

(WWW.MAGIC.CA/~GREGOR/QUOTES.HTML)

Harris is struggling to overcome his image as "Chainsaw Mike," as he's been dubbed by Premier Bob Rae.

"I'm a sensitive person," he said yesterday. "I hurt. I care."

But he said he expects "vicious personal attacks" to continue.

(*Toronto Star*, 20 November 1996)

11

MR. SILLY'S FRIEND

Premier Mike Harris yesterday slammed a prestigious literary publishing company as a corporate welfare bum, saying taxpayers should not subsidize a profit-making company.

"Unfortunately, we have a history of complete government dependency almost in Ontario and we are trying to change that," Harris told reporters when questioned about the demise of Coach House Press. "We are prepared to do our share, but we would sooner see our share go in such a way as it's more directly to the artists than it is to a profit-making company that depends on government taxpayers' dollars to compete," he said.

"If they can't compete in the marketplace . . . if their reaction is to blame somebody else, that probably speaks to their management capabilities," Harris told reporters.

(*Toronto Star*, 17 July 1996)

Speaking to reporters yesterday, Mr. Harris insisted he has never supported benefits for same-sex couples.

"We clearly oppose, as a priority, the extension of same-sex benefits.… We've taken the same position in both by-elections."

During the campaign for a by-election on 2 April 1993 in the downtown Toronto riding of St. George-St. David, which has a high homosexual population, candidates from all three main parties promised to fight for same-sex benefits.

Conservative candidate Nancy Jackman told voters, "My leader, Mike Harris, is encouraging me to work to redefine the term 'spouse' in all legislation. It must include a wider range of individuals in committed, supportive relationships, including same-sex couples."

But Mr. Harris insisted yesterday he refused to hold a news conference to support Ms. Jackman's stand.

"I said no, that is not the priority for our caucus. We called for an examination of the whole benefit plan, but we said clearly we would not change the definition of spouse." ☞

One might say that was just Ms. Jackman talking, not Mr. Harris. But on the same pamphlet was a list of testimonials. One of them came from Mr. Harris: "Nancy Jackman has done more to support policy measures concerning AIDS, same-sex spousal benefits and equity issues than any member of the Liberal-NDP governments of the past eight years. I look forward to her continued and direct involvement on these issues as the next MPP for St. George-St. David."

(*Hamilton Spectator*, 17 March 1994)

"I'm not a bookworm or a Rhodes Scholar," he says, contrasting himself with the Oxford-educated Rae. When it comes to his taste in movies, Harris says, "I'm looking to be entertained, not to be taught anything."

(*Macleans*, 15 May, 1995)

"What is my favourite book? Uh, probably, uh, uh, I'm trying to, yeah, you've caught me here, I wasn't ready for this."

Now, scrummers are by nature a sympathetic lot and tried to help him out, lobbing up the title of his campaign pamphlet, *The Common Sense Revolution*.

"Thanks very much. *The Common Sense Revolution* ranks very high up there. I don't know. Lately, uh, uh, I guess it's, uh, there's been a book called *Mr. Silly*."

Here the pounding hearts of advisers became audible.

"And it's one of [his son] Jeffrey's favourites and one of my favourites and I wish I could give you the author, but there's a series of books written by the author and they're some of Jeffrey's favourites. Most of the books I read now are kids' books."

We're already at the scrum. The reporter who raised the matter pressed on, asking Harris what was his favourite book of all time. ☞

"I don't have one clear favourite. I mean, I love reading. As a boy, I mean, I read all The Hardy Boy books. I read the sports books. I read *He Shoots, He Scores*, was an all-time favourite of mine through teen years, you know a hockey book. I think it was about the Maple Leafs, Teeder Kennedy and all those heroes of my day. But I don't think I have a single favourite."

(*Ottawa Citizen*, 25 April 1997)

When the same question [about what book he is reading] was asked yesterday, he was quick to respond that the previous evening he had been reading *Golf is an Easy Game*. "It has absolutely nothing to do with golf and all to do with thinking."

But the embarrassment over the *Mr. Silly* episode was not a total loss, he said. "Jeffrey got some benefit out of it," he said, explaining, "I got some [children's] books sent to me that were by Canadian authors."

(*Globe and Mail*, 7 June 1997)

In May, the Ontario government announced it had reduced OAC funding by 16.5 percent, on top of the 10 percent cut in 1995–96 and the 18.6 percent cut in 1996–97. In just eighteen months, our budget plummeted from $42.6 million (1995–96) to $25.3 million for this fiscal year. Provincial government support to artists and arts organizations through OAC now stands at 1974/75 levels, taking into account the effects of inflation.

(*Ontario Arts Council Bulletin*, 15 July 1997)

TAKE-ME-TO-YOUR-LEADER MIKE

According to Deane Harris, Mike's father: "Running the province is no different than running a pro shop."

(*Maclean's*, 19 June 1995)

MIKE HARRIS: There is not a single cut in any of the cultural grants, in any of that pot of pie that is there.

CBLT: Is that an absolute commitment? You will not cut cultural grants?

MIKE HARRIS: Yes, it is. (30 May 1995)

(*Culture Matters in Ontario* Newsletter, April 1997)

Premier Mike Harris said there is nothing wrong with the Progressive Conservative party footing the bill for such things as his personal clothes, golfing fees, and private club dues.

"This has nothing to do with taxpayers' money," Harris told the Legislature after opposition MPPs accused him of abusing tax-deductible donations to his riding association.

In 1994, Harris claimed at least $18,000 in personal expenses from the riding association, including $7,260 to upgrade his Toronto accommodation, $5,113 in petty cash, $2,281 for meals and entertaining, $1,047 for dues and fees at the North Bay Golf and Country Club and $996 for dry cleaning.

(*Toronto Star*, 18–19 April 1996)

Opposition members demanded yesterday that Harris attend a Queen's Park committee to explain the massive implications of Bill 26, which runs more than 2,000 pages, changes more than 47 Ontario laws, and creates some new laws.

"I'm not going to appear because I think they're in the technical parts of clause-by-clause [hearings] of the bill and I'm not an expert in that," he told reporters yesterday.

"I'll be happy to explain [it] to you in the Legislature [on Monday]," Harris said yesterday, referring to debate before the vote on the bill's passage.

(Toronto Star, 25 January 1996)

About 400 members of the right-wing National Citizens' Coalition last night lavished praise, standing ovations, and their highest award on Harris for slashing spending and getting government out of the way of personal freedom.

"Mike Harris is walking through our public life carrying a load that weighs 100,000 pounds without ever letting his back sag, without ever letting the burden seem heavy, without ever ceasing to smile," neo-conservative commentator David Frum told the cheering crowd.

"I can't believe it. Just two weekends ago a great parade from labour and now this," Harris joked about the Metro Days of Action.

(*Toronto Star*, 5 November 1996)

25

SOLIDARITY MIKE

Ontario Premier Mike Harris yesterday casually derided the tens of thousands of protesters who had demonstrated against him the day before.

"If you took away all the government employees, the other four or five had a point to make," he joked at a question-and-answer session with Tory convention delegates that he thought was free of reporters. The party faithful roared.

Harris also made light of the fact that police reports put Saturday's crowd at 75,000, a quarter of what protest organizers claimed.

Talking to the 500 delegates, he said "It's great to look out and see 35,000 people."

Harris went on to say that "by and large, I think the main-stream [marchers] were union-organized." ☞

He made the comments when asked by a reporter whether the parade included special-interest groups he had earlier vowed to ignore.

"They are a lot of special-interest groups," he replied.

"If you saw the banners going by from some of the Communist parties, as I saw, and I guess the Iraqi group [and] Iranian group. . . . Clearly those who've not found work yet have no reason in their own family lives to say, 'Boy, we're better off.'"

(Maclean's, 15 May 1995)

Premier Mike Harris has issued a written apology to an Arab group for his comments Saturday about the Metro Days of Action protest and march.

His office received a letter of complaint yesterday from the Canadian Arab Federation, calling the comments racist and demanding an apology.

"Please be assured, it was not my intention to single out or denigrate any specific group," Harris wrote to the federation. ☞

"If my remarks, or the interpretation of them, have caused offence, please accept my apologies."

Yesterday, Harris said, "If Saturday, I referenced the fact there were delegations from both Iraqi Canadians and Iranian Canadians, I may have said that. I didn't mean to offend anybody. I didn't want to leave anybody out," he told reporters before the written apology was issued.

(Toronto Star, 31 October 1996)

Calling the protesters in Hamilton "union goons," Harris told the PC crowd that "I am delighted to be here with you for dinner tonight. Although, I really couldn't leave the hotel even if I wanted to. . . . No union-led demonstration will deter us. And no editorial . . . will dissuade us."

When someone asked if he ordered the police presence, he shot back, sarcastically: "I don't control the police. You see, that's the great thing about a parliamentary democracy — the separation between the police and the state."

(Canadian Dimension, May–June 1996)

"You and I know that those people parading on the streets today do not have a monopoly on compassion. . . . The difference is, the people in this room have the ideas to lead Ontario back to prosperity and to the rightful place in Canada that this province deserves."

(Toronto Star, 25 February 1996)

31

MEGA-CITY MIKE

"Let me put it into perspective. I don't want to diminish, that's why we're listening, taking our time and making changes to the proposed legislation. On the night of the 'so-called' referendum, there was a big celebration with 2,000 or 3,000 people and everything else, while down the street there were 12,000 for the opening of Planet Hollywood. So it didn't exactly take the city by storm."

(*This*, July/August 1997)

Mega-City Mike: "I think this is a desperation call to save their own jobs by people who've always been opposed to referendums and don't understand them. I think it will be money wasted."

"I mean, they [Metro Toronto residents] have the status quo. . . . They want to put the status quo on the ballot. But the status quo is not acceptable. . . . This is a political ploy, some kind of desperate grab, and the taxpayers are going to have to pay for it. I don't think that's good government."

He said Toronto's municipal politicians have opposed referendums for some time. "We think this is far too little too late."

Furious Liberal MPP Mike Colle (Oakwood), a former Metro councillor, accused the government of acting like a dictatorship.

"Where did you get the right to suspend democracy and ram this down the throats of the citizens of Metro?" he demanded in the Legislature.

(*Toronto Star*, 19 December 1996)

"I don't think the average Ontarian, when it comes to government services, will see or feel very much," the Premier said.

"But for somebody involved in the actual delivery of the service, there could be a change. A garbage collector who is currently working for a municipality, three years from now may be working for a company or a different municipality or different structure."

Senior Conservatives say the first round of cuts, while not easy, was the "low hanging fruit" of government waste and was obvious for the picking. Those sources say the next $3 billion in cuts will be much more difficult.

Harris said the provincial government bureaucracy "was so big and bloated and fat" that the $8 billion in cuts can be made without affecting "first-class quality services."

"At the end of the day, people will get the services; garbage will be picked up, kids will be taught in school, and health care services will be there. But there may be fewer public-sector workers." ☞

"This can be quite traumatic for them and for their families." . . . The Premier admitted that some of the first round of $5 billion in cuts have caused "transition difficulties" the government never intended.

(Toronto Star, 1 November 1996)

SPIN-DOCTOR MIKE

Premier Mike Harris was forced to make an embarrassing apology yesterday to Gerard Kennedy, executive director of the Daily Bread Food Bank, for an attack he made on Kennedy during a television show this week.

On Thursday's TVOntario newsmagazine show *Studio 2*, Harris was asked about Kennedy's comments regarding the disturbing fact that reliance on food banks is up more than 50 percent from a year ago.

Harris retorted angrily: "This is the same guy that campaigned and helped destroy us bringing the Olympics to Toronto which would have created a massive number of jobs in Toronto. So, philosophically, I think had we done a lot of things differently the last 10 years we wouldn't need a Gerard Kennedy or a food bank and I regret that we do," he said on TVOntario.

Problem is, the Premier was mistaken. ☞

Kennedy pointed out in a letter to Harris yesterday that it was not the Daily Bread Food Bank which opposed the Olympic bid, but in fact the organization Bread Not Circuses (led by social activist Michael Shapcott).

During the Olympic bid, Kennedy said, he actually served on a committee promoting a parallel Expo 2000 bid, alongside such Progressive Conservative party bigwigs as former premier William Davis and strategist John Tory.

Kennedy told Harris his comments would be "harmful" to the food bank's spring drive.

Kennedy asked for a clarification from the Premier, and asked that he visit the Daily Bread Food Bank soon to help promote the spring food drive. He also asked that Harris consider meeting with him to discuss a report on Ontario food banks to be released next week.

"Please accept my personal apology for the mistake I made on TVOntario's *Studio 2*," Harris wrote to Kennedy in a letter released late yesterday. ☞

"Quite clearly, I was wrong to identify you and your organization as participating in the Bread Not Circuses coalition's campaign," the Premier wrote.

Harris added he always supports volunteerism and "I respect the work done by you. . . . I do believe we share a mutual goal of doing everything we can to eliminate the need for food banks."

(*Toronto Star*, 30 March 1996)

On Ipperwash OPP shooting: "Was I involved in informal meetings? I don't know what an informal meeting is. When I go to bed at night, is that an informal meeting?"

(*Hansard*, 29 May 1996)

"Just as Hula-Hoops went out and those workers had to have a factory and a company that would manufacture something else that's in, it's the same in government, and you know, governments have put off these decisions for so many years that restructuring sometimes is painful."

(*Globe and Mail*, 5 March 1997)

"If the Hula-Hoop analogy offends any, of course, I apologize. . . . Perhaps I'd have been better to use the analogy that the head of the North York General used talking about railways, that times have changed and transportation needs have changed and restructuring must go on."

(*Globe and Mail*, 6 March 1997)

ROBERT FISHER: In other provinces, hospitals are being closed as governments struggle with their debt. Therefore, can you guarantee us tonight that your pledge to protect services will mean that you will not close hospitals?

MIKE HARRIS: Certainly, I can guarantee you, Robert, that it is not my plan to close hospitals.

(Transcript of Leaders' Debate, 18 May 1995)

"There will be a number of specialists who would say that the facilities at Sunnybrook [Health Science Centre] will be far better, will be able to treat women far better, that women's health care is not dependent upon a dingy old building, that is rather old, in downtown Toronto."

(*Globe and Mail*, 24 July 1997)

"I would look at the federal election this way: 89 percent of Ontarians voted for parties that said, 'We're going to downsize government, we're going to balance the budget, and we're going to cut taxes. . . . I would say that 89 percent of the people voted for the policies that I am fighting for and the changes we're bringing to the province of Ontario."

(*Globe and Mail*, 7 June 1997)

AMBASSADOR MIKE

"We're declining as a country. In fact, I am one who believes we're pretty close to the brink of collapse."

(*The Globe and Mail*, 28 October 1994)

Tory leader Mike Harris says he "makes no apologies" for hiring two Americans to help sell his common sense revolution in Ontario.

But at least one group of Metro workers thinks Harris makes no sense at all.

The Association of Canadian Film Craftspeople said Toronto is one of the largest film and video production centres in North America, and the hiring of Americans is an insult.

Harris — who was on the first day of a southwestern Ontario campaign-style swing — defended hiring the U.S. director and New York cameraman to shoot the television ads for his $600,000 pre-election blueprint.

"I'm a free-trader," he said. "We're after the best and the brightest around the world." ☞

Harris said the director of the 30-second television ads — which depict Ontario as a place of economic gloom and doom crying out for his leadership — is a personal friend of Conservative campaign chairman Tom Long.

"[And] the cameraman was an American the director liked to work with," he said.

Harris couldn't say if the rest of the team was all-Canadian.

"I don't know. I didn't check passports."

(Toronto Star, 10 May 1994)

There is "zero" chance of Quebec separating from Canada, Ontario Premier Mike Harris has told a U.S. business and investment audience. "I think the chances of a separation between Quebec and Canada are zilch, absolutely zero. I don't see any possibility," Harris told a Manhattan luncheon audience of 250.

He said it is "my own personal view and I freely admit that it is not shared by everyone in Canada. There are some political experts who [don't agree], the same ones who never thought I'd win in Ontario."

(*Toronto Star*, 7 June 1996)

GREEN MIKE

Harris on pollution: "We have done a lot but not enough."

(Windsor Star, 10 June 1997).

Despite massive environmental cutbacks, Ontario Premier Mike Harris says his government is merely eliminating "silly and unenforceable rules" and not giving businesses a licence to pollute. . . .

"We need to challenge the assumption that the more money we spend, the more regulations we have on the books and the more people we have in bureaucracy means more progress in protecting the environment," Harris told a green technologies conference sponsored by the environment ministry.

(Toronto Star, 14 November 1996)

An industry spokesperson told the conference the government's willingness to allow companies to take voluntary measures to reduce pollution was a welcome change.

(*Toronto Star*, 14 November 1996)

New Tory Premier Mike Harris can't wait to get the chainsaws ripping down the trees — some of them hundreds of years old — of Northern Ontario's prized Temagami wilderness area.

He's also impatient to mine the 10,000-square-kilometre area north of his North Bay home.

Last week, Harris said it's taken too long to end a development freeze for Temagami. He contended: "We're very concerned with how long it is taking. We want to get exploration going and development going so that there's jobs for native and non-natives alike."

(*Toronto Sun*, 30 July 1995)

MIKEY CLONES

"We'll take a look, certainly when the house recesses, at reviewing where we're at on personnel in cabinet," Harris told the *Star*.

(Toronto Star, 1 June 1996)

David Tsubouchi will be retained in cabinet, although probably in another post. Among his many gaffes, Tsubouchi told welfare recipients to bargain on cans of tuna after he cut their benefits 21.6 percent.

(Toronto Star, 1 June 1996)

John Snobelen: "Yeah, we need to invent a crisis and that's not just an act of courage, there's some skill involved."

(Toronto Star, 12 September 1995)

Al Leach, then Minister of Housing: "I know about as much about housing as you can put on the head of a pin and still have room left over for the Lord's Prayer."

(Globe and Mail, 26 August 1995)

What Canadian movies has Ontario Culture Minister Marilyn Mushinski seen? "My daughter got me to watch *Mortal Beloved*. It's about a composer (Beethoven, and its actual title is *Immortal Beloved*). I guess that's not Canadian."

"I want you to know my ministry is very important to me. Culture is extremely important to me. Culture is extremely important. It's not a frills ministry. There is not a government in the Western world that doesn't have a ministry of culture."

(*Toronto Star*, 5 May 1996)

Al Palladini, Minister of Transportation, referring to possible cuts to Ministers' limos: "Fighting the traffic to come downtown, I'm not used to. I wouldn't want to do it every day. It's rough. There are percs that have been around."

(*Toronto Sun*, 6 July 1995)

Conservative backbencher Joe Spina (Brampton North) allegedly yelled "Speak English" at New Democrat MPP Gilles Bisson as Bisson spoke in French on Monday about the 10th anniversary of Bill 8, the province's French Language Services Act.

(*Toronto Star*, 20 November 1996)

Al Palladini: "Right now, all we basically have is a bridge that we quite don't know how to walk across it. Once we know what it's going to take to walk across it, we might need one paddle, we might need two. I'm going to leave the door wide open."

(*Ottawa Citizen*, 17 April 1996)

Al Leach defends the Omnibus Bill: "I had that right there to read back to you. Completely lost. . . . Mr. Speaker, give me two minutes. . . . That's another one I'm going to take under advisement."

(*Ontario Legislature*, 12 December 1995)

Asked if he feels it is okay to defraud Ford Motor Company on warranty deals if Ford doesn't catch on, Palladini responded, "Well, if the customer benefits, obviously, I am okay with it."

Sensing an easy kill, Kormos waded into the debate suggesting that Al's remarks were unworthy of a member of the legislature. Later, a Park hack asked Palladini if he had any response to Kormos. "If he had any balls," replied Al, "he'd say it to my face."

The next day, Kormos summoned a parliamentary page to deliver two tennis balls in a plain brown paper bag to Palladini's office.

Palladini then sent the page back to Kormos, bag in hand, with instructions to tell Kormos to "shove them up his ass."

Another duel of wits between unarmed men.

(*Frank*, 3 July 1996)

Snobelen: "The whole idea of an invented crisis, I guess the word sounds a little strange if you were to literally define it."

(*Toronto Star*, 13 September 1995)

Snobelen: "Using the word invention wasn't very smart. I certainly regret using the word invent in the way it's been interpreted."

(*Toronto Sun*, 14 September 1995)

"We are getting feedback that perhaps we are moving too quickly," said Tony Skarica (Wentworth North), a Tory backbencher who has often criticized the government since being fired from his parliamentary assistant's post in April.

"We're obviously on the downward slide and there's a point when you get so far down you can never come back," Skarica said outside the caucus meeting.

Harris told reporters some Tory caucus members are more critical than others, based, he said, "on my judgment of who is and is not in cabinet."

(*Toronto Star*, 20 August 1997)

Morley Kells, MPP Etobicoke-Lakeshore: "Apparently, it's starting to dawn on many Ontarians that they are neither sharing in the good times, nor gaining monetary improvement from all the changes coming at them in a wave.

"Yet, it must be remembered that the direction of this administration resides almost totally in the hands of the political operators in the Premier's office."

(Toronto Star, 30 August 1997)

Mike Harris: "I think it's reasonable that politicians who campaign in a direction or on a platform for things that are within their control, that they ought to resign or go back to the people if they in fact are going to change their minds."

(Toronto Star, 2 May 1995)

RESUME

1945   Born in Toronto

1963   Algonquin Composite School yearbook lists his pastimes as "bowling, curling, and antagonizing." The crew-cut 17-year-old was known as "Mikey" or "Hairy Harris."

1965   Enrols in Waterloo Lutheran University (now Wilfrid Laurier University) to major in math and science. Drops out.

1966–68   Works as a ski instructor in Quebec; returns to North Bay, spends a year in teacher's college. Begins teaching math and science in a public school.

1971   Leaves teaching, becomes a golf pro and manager.

1974   Elected to the local school board; elected chair.

1995   Elected premier of Ontario.